Daily Thanks

THE YEAR-ROUND
GRATITUDE JOURNAL

Published by Familius LLC, www.familius.com
1254 Commerce Way, Sanger, CA 93657

Familius books are available at special discounts for bulk purchases, whether
for sales promotions or for family or corporate use. For more information,
contact Familius Sales at 559-876-2170 or email orders@familius.com.

Library of Congress Control Number: 9781641703185
Print ISBN 9781641703185

Printed in China

Cover design by Brooke Jorden
Book design by Mara Harris

10 9 8 7 6 5 4 3 2 1

First Edition

GRATITUDE DOESN'T LEAD TO HAPPINESS.
Gratitude is happiness
IN ITS MOST OBTAINABLE FORM.

INTRODUCTION

MOST people acknowledge the connection between thankfulness and happiness. We take it a step further: *Gratitude is more than a path to happiness. Gratitude IS happiness in its most obtainable form.*

Almost 40 years ago, we decided to stop sending Christmas cards and start sending Thanksgiving cards* instead. We felt that thankfulness was the best way to appreciate the year past and the perfect entrée to the Christmas season.

As we raised our children, we tried to show them the magic and joy of gratitude, and one of our methods was the keeping of gratitude journals. We would start off each year determined to make a journal entry every day, but as the year went on, we became less diligent on this specific daily thankfulness. Then we discovered that by focusing on a different type of gratitude each month, we were able to stay with it and find a fresh thankfulness entry each day for our journals.

We incorporated that idea into this book, and we hope that each month during this coming year, you will find a new awareness of blessings as you record them daily in this journal. We hope you will discover new approaches and perspectives and dimensions to your gratitude—and with them, a deeper, more consistent happiness and contentment in your soul.

  —Richard and Linda Eyre
   Park City, Utah, 2020 (the year of clear vision)

*You can view all the Eyres' Thanksgiving greeting cards from the last 40 years at www.valuesparenting.com/thanksgiving, and can go on their mailing list to receive their new card each year in November.

NOVEMBER

Remembrance

THERE are certain perfect late-autumn days that
Lend themselves to reflection and remembering.
The certainty of winter induces fond recall
Of longer, warmer days, and
The sky spreads wide like a mackerel memory,
Its bright scales revealing the reeds of past deeds,
The peace of earlier release.
As we approach the holiday that is
Named after the synonym for happiness,
The build-up should be about remembering.
The year now winding down, we look back
And recall how much has been given us,
And how little we deserve it.

Remembering may be the precise opposite
Of taking-for-granted.
Some say that remembering is the consummate skill.
When we remember,
We don't have to learn the same facts,
Or the same lessons, or the same abilities
All over again.
When we remember,
We return favors and thank people for small things.
When we remember, it makes God bigger
And ourselves comfortably, securely smaller.

When we remember moments of joy,
The moments are twice felt.
When we remember error,
We are less likely to repeat it.
When we remember love, it is nourished and grows.
When we remember peace,
We also remember where to find it.

And when we remember gratitude, it overflows,
Leaving us warmed and filled.

We nurture and care for our gratitude by remembering,
Negotiating the curbs and trips of takeforgranted
That could spill the beauty from the buggy.

There are many ways to remember to be grateful,
The best one being prayer.
Pray oftener,
And give equal content-weight to prayer's two sides:
Thanking and Asking.

Remembering is both a bridge and a mirror,
Showing us where and who we are
and who we have become.

These are good things to think about
As the year winds down,
And the grace of Christmas ramps up.

THE CHALLENGE

AS Thanksgiving approaches, start a list
Of thankful things big and small. Number it.
List at least ten every day.
1. Sunsets
2. Doorknobs
3. A mother's love
4. Etc. . . .

It may range from the petty to the profound.
On Thanksgiving morning, while the turkey cooks,
Build the list. Get everyone involved.
See if you can get to 100, 200, 500 . . .

Think for a moment about each one,
About why you are happy to have it.
Let each tiny twinge of gratitude
Collect in your list to help you
REMEMBER.

NOVEMBER 1

1. _____
2. _____
3. _____
4. _____
5. _____
6. _____
7. _____
8. _____
9. _____
10. _____

NOVEMBER 2

1. _____
2. _____
3. _____
4. _____
5. _____
6. _____
7. _____
8. _____
9. _____
10. _____

"THE ESSENCE OF ALL BEAUTIFUL ART, ALL GREAT ART, IS *gratitude.*"

FRIEDRICH
NIETZSCHE

NOVEMBER 3

1.
2.
3.
4.
5.
6.
7.
8.
9.
10.

NOVEMBER 4

1.
2.
3.
4.
5.
6.
7.
8.
9.
10.

NOVEMBER 5

1. _____
2. _____
3. _____
4. _____
5. _____
6. _____
7. _____
8. _____
9. _____
10. _____

NOVEMBER 6

1. _____
2. _____
3. _____
4. _____
5. _____
6. _____
7. _____
8. _____
9. _____
10. _____

"CLEARLY, ONE OF THE MAJOR OBSTACLES TO OUR EXPERIENCE OF GRATITUDE IS THE HABIT WE HAVE OF *sleepwalking through life.* THE TRUTH IS THAT WE ARE NEVER LACKING FOR BLESSINGS IN OUR LIVES, BUT WE ARE OFTEN LACKING IN AWARENESS AND RECOGNITION OF THEM."

DIANE BERKE, PHD

NOVEMBER 7

1.
2.
3.
4.
5.
6.
7.
8.
9.
10.

NOVEMBER 8

1.
2.
3.
4.
5.
6.
7.
8.
9.
10.

NOVEMBER 9

1. _____
2. _____
3. _____
4. _____
5. _____
6. _____
7. _____
8. _____
9. _____
10. _____

NOVEMBER 10

1. _____
2. _____
3. _____
4. _____
5. _____
6. _____
7. _____
8. _____
9. _____
10. _____

NOVEMBER 11

1.
2.
3.
4.
5.
6.
7.
8.
9.
10.

NOVEMBER 12

1.
2.
3.
4.
5.
6.
7.
8.
9.
10.

NOVEMBER 13

1.
2.
3.
4.
5.
6.
7.
8.
9.
10.

NOVEMBER 14

1.
2.
3.
4.
5.
6.
7.
8.
9.
10.

NOVEMBER 15

1. _____
2. _____
3. _____
4. _____
5. _____
6. _____
7. _____
8. _____
9. _____
10. _____

NOVEMBER 16

1. _____
2. _____
3. _____
4. _____
5. _____
6. _____
7. _____
8. _____
9. _____
10. _____

"PERHAPS NOTHING HELPS US MAKE THE MOVEMENT FROM OUR LITTLE SELVES TO A LARGER WORLD THAN *remembering God* IN GRATITUDE."

HENRI NOUWEN

NOVEMBER 17

1.
2.
3.
4.
5.
6.
7.
8.
9.
10.

NOVEMBER 18

1.
2.
3.
4.
5.
6.
7.
8.
9.
10.

NOVEMBER 19

1.
2.
3.
4.
5.
6.
7.
8.
9.
10.

NOVEMBER 20

1.
2.
3.
4.
5.
6.
7.
8.
9.
10.

"THE MOST FORTUNATE ARE THOSE WHO HAVE A WONDERFUL CAPACITY TO APPRECIATE AGAIN AND AGAIN, FRESHLY AND NAIVELY, THE BASIC GOODS OF LIFE, WITH

awe, pleasure, wonder, and even ecstasy."

ABRAHAM MASLOW

NOVEMBER 21

1.
2.
3.
4.
5.
6.
7.
8.
9.
10.

NOVEMBER 22

1.
2.
3.
4.
5.
6.
7.
8.
9.
10.

NOVEMBER 23

1.
2.
3.
4.
5.
6.
7.
8.
9.
10.

NOVEMBER 24

1.
2.
3.
4.
5.
6.
7.
8.
9.
10.

"To look backward
FOR A WHILE IS TO REFRESH THE EYE,
TO RESTORE IT, AND TO RENDER IT THE
MORE FIT FOR ITS PRIME FUNCTION
of looking forward."

MARGARET FAIRLESS BARBER,
THE ROADMENDER

NOVEMBER 25

1.
2.
3.
4.
5.
6.
7.
8.
9.
10.

NOVEMBER 26

1.
2.
3.
4.
5.
6.
7.
8.
9.
10.

NOVEMBER 27

1. _____
2. _____
3. _____
4. _____
5. _____
6. _____
7. _____
8. _____
9. _____
10. _____

NOVEMBER 28

1. _____
2. _____
3. _____
4. _____
5. _____
6. _____
7. _____
8. _____
9. _____
10. _____

NOVEMBER 29

1.
2.
3.
4.
5.
6.
7.
8.
9.
10.

NOVEMBER 30

1.
2.
3.
4.
5.
6.
7.
8.
9.
10.

DECEMBER

Grace

PERHAPS gratitude, grace, and joy
All begin with beauty.
Keats said, "A thing of beauty is a joy forever,"
And then he upped the ante by saying,
"Beauty is truth, truth beauty.
That is all ye know on earth,
And all ye need to know."
In the rant and rush of pushy life,
We need to find the moments,
To see beauty,
To sit peacefully and feel our thoughts,
And soak in the gratitude and grace and joy.

Grace and Gratitude go together,
Not only in their alliteration,
But in their root—both come from the Latin *gratia*
Meaning "grace, graciousness, or gratefulness."

Grace is the ultimate gratitude to the Ultimate Giver.
If thanks just lies there, naked and inert,
It will probably fossilize and turn hard and brittle.
By itself it is unconnected
And spinning in its own lonely orbit.
It needs to be applied to something
And extended to someone.

To say "I'm thankful" as an observation is one thing,
But to point and say "I'm thankful" for that blessing
And to let a little place in you turn warm and quiver a bit
With the beauty of it . . .
That is thankfulness with an object.

Still, without a recipient or a subject,
The thanks is sterile and undirected,
Destined to fly onward through space
Without an end or a destination—
A circuit without a current,
An expression without a connection.

But to say "I'm thankful" to the giver completes the circuit
And turns on the light,
Especially if the Giver is God and the Light is His Spirit.

Christmas, the wave of beauty and peace,
The celebration of the birth of stunning sacrifice . . .
We are as a tiny naked babe staring up and
Trying to grasp the grandeur of His grace.

"Grace-full-ness"
Amazing Grace
Beyond amazing, grace is
Miraculously mysterious because
It is the magic of One Spirit's singular perfection
Overcoming the vast imperfections of the other billions.
We can't comprehend it, but we can appreciate it
And be awed by it.
And peace somehow interprets itself within us,
Changing us, transforming us, gradually gifting grace
Until we become grace-full and grateful,
A beauty from within.

Gratitude plays a place in the transformation—
Growing, gathering perspective and awareness,
Deepening and permeating and in a way overwhelming us
Into realizing that it is actually too big
For mere appreciation to comprehend.

Evolving, elevating, energizing,
A progressing process whereby gratitude turns to awe
And finally to grace.
And we emerge amazed and awe-struck and saved.
Gratitude beyond gratitude!

The Biblical Paul taught us that it is by grace (God's gift)
That we are saved, after all we can do.

THE CHALLENGE

HOWEVER you pray, add more thanks-giving.
Thank God for 5 new things each night.
In this book, keep a list for the month—
"The 31 days of Christmas."

Then, on New Year's Eve, inventory all 155.

DECEMBER 1

1. _____

2. _____

3. _____

4. _____

5. _____

DECEMBER 2

1. _____

2. _____

3. _____

4. _____

5. _____

"MOST HUMAN BEINGS
HAVE AN ALMOST INFINITE
CAPACITY FOR TAKING
THINGS FOR GRANTED."

ALDOUS HUXLEY

DECEMBER 3

1.

2.

3.

4.

5.

DECEMBER 4

1.

2.

3.

4.

5.

DECEMBER 5

1. _____

2. _____

3. _____

4. _____

5. _____

DECEMBER 6

1. _____

2. _____

3. _____

4. _____

5. _____

"GRACE ISN'T A LITTLE PRAYER
YOU CHANT BEFORE
RECEIVING A MEAL.
It's a way to live."

JACQUELINE WINSPEAR

DECEMBER 7

1. _____

2. _____

3. _____

4. _____

5. _____

DECEMBER 8

1. _____

2. _____

3. _____

4. _____

5. _____

DECEMBER 9

1. _____
_____

2. _____
_____

3. _____
_____

4. _____
_____

5. _____
_____

DECEMBER 10

1. _____
_____

2. _____
_____

3. _____
_____

4. _____
_____

5. _____
_____

DECEMBER 11

1.

2.

3.

4.

5.

DECEMBER 12

1.

2.

3.

4.

5.

DECEMBER 13

1. _____

2. _____

3. _____

4. _____

5. _____

DECEMBER 14

1. _____

2. _____

3. _____

4. _____

5. _____

DECEMBER 15

1.

2.

3.

4.

5.

DECEMBER 16

1.

2.

3.

4.

5.

"WHEN WE WERE CHILDREN
we were grateful
TO THOSE WHO FILLED OUR STOCKINGS
AT CHRISTMAS TIME. WHY ARE WE NOT
GRATEFUL TO GOD FOR FILLING OUR
STOCKINGS WITH LEGS?"

G. K. CHESTERTON

DECEMBER 17

1. _____

2. _____

3. _____

4. _____

5. _____

DECEMBER 18

1. _____

2. _____

3. _____

4. _____

5. _____

DECEMBER 19

1.

2.

3.

4.

5.

DECEMBER 20

1.

2.

3.

4.

5.

DECEMBER 21

1. _____

_____

2. _____

_____

3. _____

_____

4. _____

_____

5. _____

_____

DECEMBER 22

1. _____

_____

2. _____

_____

3. _____

_____

4. _____

_____

5. _____

_____

IT IS ALL FOR YOUR SAKE, SO THAT AS GRACE EXTENDS TO MORE AND MORE PEOPLE IT MAY INCREASE THANKSGIVING, *to the glory of God.*

2 CORINTHIANS 4:15

DECEMBER 23

1.

2.

3.

4.

5.

DECEMBER 24

1.

2.

3.

4.

5.

DECEMBER 25

1.

2.

3.

4.

5.

DECEMBER 26

1.

2.

3.

4.

5.

DECEMBER 27

1.

2.

3.

4.

5.

DECEMBER 28

1.

2.

3.

4.

5.

DECEMBER 29

1. _____

2. _____

3. _____

4. _____

5. _____

DECEMBER 30

1. _____

2. _____

3. _____

4. _____

5. _____

DECEMBER 31

1. _____

_____

2. _____

_____

3. _____

_____

4. _____

_____

5. _____

_____

INVENTORY ALL 155 THINGS YOU
WROTE THROUGHOUT THE MONTH
AND REFLECT ON GOD'S GRACE

JANUARY

Perspective

OUR seeing is improved,
Not so much by a new ocular prescription
As by increasing awareness and perspective.
With deliberate effort, we can open our minds to light
And become as one bird, alight, but with winged heart,
Feeling the world all around and able to fly up
And see it all from above.

Can you state the difference between man and God
In two words?
Is to ask, or to try, blasphemous?
If we did attempt, the two words might be:
Awareness and Perspective.
We see such a narrow slice, a sliver really,
God sees all.
Our perspective is earthly and mortal,
His is eternal and perfect.

What saves us is awareness and our perspective
And both are expandable
And we sense that, as His children,
We have infinitely more in common than different.

Awareness . . .
We have five senses, and use only a fraction of each.
And a sixth, in the soul, often dormant
But always summon-able.

Were we all more aware, we would all be more grateful,
For awareness is the sense and perception
Of what is around us and in us,
And the epiphany that all of both come from God.
Those who see that, who really see it,
Also see God.
The shortest perspective is
Eat, drink, and be merry,
But that kind of merriness never turns to joy.

A middle perspective is duty,
And while it keeps commandments and follows laws,
It does not, now or ever, exalt the soul.

The longest perspective is eternity,
And oh how that perspective changes us.
Extending our view from finite to infinite, letting us
See suddenly that we are not growing up from the earth,
But hanging down from the sky.

A two-way eternity, not only forever forward,
But forever back into pre-mortal life
Where we, full of perspective,
Shouted for joy at the prospect
Of coming to this physical place
To struggle and fumble and fizzle and fail
But to learn from it all, to progress in ways not possible
Until body and agency and families of our own
Made us more like God.

That perspective precipitates and promotes and produces
Gratitude.
How could it not, because it presupposes a Father-God
Who wants to give us all He has.

THE CHALLENGE

WAKE up!
Notice more!
Take more in!
Spend less time inside yourself, worrying,
And more time outside yourself, rejoicing.

If you have troubles, see through them.
If you have challenges, see over them.
If you have blessings, see God's hand in them.

This month, taste, smell, look, and listen harder,
And feel more, with both your skin and your soul.
Each day, write down one new thing
That one of your senses revealed to you.

And let your increasing awareness give you
The perspective
That catalyzes gratitude.

"WAKE AT DAWN WITH A WINGED HEART AND GIVE THANKS FOR another day of loving."

KAHLIL GIBRAN

JANUARY 1

JANUARY 2

JANUARY 3

JANUARY 4

"WE CAN ONLY BE SAID TO *be alive in those moments* WHEN OUR HEARTS ARE CONSCIOUS OF OUR TREASURES."

THORNTON WILDER

JANUARY 5

JANUARY 6

JANUARY 7

JANUARY 8

JANUARY 9

JANUARY 10

JANUARY 11

JANUARY 12

JANUARY 13

JANUARY 14

IN EVERY THING
GIVE THANKS:
*for this is the
will of God.*

1 THESSALONIANS 5:18

JANUARY 15

JANUARY 16

JANUARY 17

JANUARY 18

JANUARY 19

JANUARY 20

"Be thankful for what you have; YOU'LL END UP HAVING MORE."

OPRAH WINFREY

JANUARY 21

JANUARY 22

JANUARY 23

JANUARY 24

"TO CHANGE OURSELVES EFFECTIVELY, WE FIRST HAD TO CHANGE OUR *perceptions.*"

STEPHEN R. COVEY

JANUARY 25

JANUARY 26

JANUARY 27

JANUARY 28

JANUARY 29

JANUARY 30

FEBRUARY

Love

CAN you look at beauty and frame it with a heart,
So that both thanks and love ride easily
Upon the seeing?
Can love and gratitude rise high in parallel planes?
So emotion's energy
Can flicker back and forth between them,
Multiplying each other like chicken and egg?

Gratitude, like love, grows every time it is given
Or received.
In fact, ask yourself,
Are Thanks-Giving and Love separable?
Can we feel one without feeling the other?
Or are they intertwined so completely
That it is impossible to tell
Where one ends and the other begins?

We all need love and we all need to give love.
We need someone to comfort us
And to hold our head when it hurts,
And when it doesn't, we need to be the holder.

Some say love is such a special word that perhaps
We should not use it so much,
On the premise that, if you try to love everything,
You will end up loving nothing

The other view is that love is such a special word
That we should use it every minute . . .
That love breeds more love and is inexhaustible
And infinitely expandable.
There are more things to love than we can ever find.
You might love one percent
Of all the things you could have loved this day
And every time you add another, gratitude grows.

You are, as one, limited and isolated;
Your slice of reality is just a sliver,
But to love others gets you into their heads
and you see what they have seen
Like entering different crystal balls,
One after another.
We need to learn to love like brothers, sisters,
And like friends,
And like parents,
And like children,
And like lovers and partners.

Here is some more magic:
As we get better at remembering blessings,
It is guaranteed
That we will also become more generous.
It is not possible to become better at receiving
Without also becoming better at giving,
Because they are two sides of one coin
And, put in motion, they spin up, feeding each other,
Catching the sun,
Reaching a higher realm of love.

THE CHALLENGE

IN this Valentine's month,
Love something or someone new each day.
A new-noticed beauty, a small opportunity,
A little convenience,
Or a person you have never loved before.

Write one in this book each day.
And write a little about that person or thing.
Many will be the same things
You have felt grateful for,
But this time, say "I love you."

FEBRUARY 1

I LOVE

_____

_____

_____

_____

_____

_____

_____

_____

_____

FEBRUARY 2

I LOVE

_____

_____

_____

_____

_____

_____

_____

_____

_____

"Love cures people—
BOTH THE ONES WHO GIVE IT
AND THE ONES WHO RECEIVE IT."

KARL MENNINGER

FEBRUARY 3

I LOVE

_____
_____
_____
_____
_____
_____
_____
_____
_____

FEBRUARY 4

I LOVE

_____
_____
_____
_____
_____
_____
_____
_____
_____

FEBRUARY 5

I LOVE

FEBRUARY 6

I LOVE

"LOVE MUST BE
AS MUCH A
light
AS IT IS A
flame."

HENRY DAVID THOREAU

FEBRUARY 7

I LOVE

FEBRUARY 8

I LOVE

FEBRUARY 9

I LOVE

_____

_____

_____

_____

_____

_____

_____

_____

_____

FEBRUARY 10

I LOVE

_____

_____

_____

_____

_____

_____

_____

_____

_____

FEBRUARY 11

I LOVE

FEBRUARY 12

I LOVE

FEBRUARY 13

I LOVE

FEBRUARY 14

I LOVE

"LOVE IS THE MASTER KEY THAT OPENS THE gates of happiness."

OLIVER WENDELL HOLMES

FEBRUARY 15

I LOVE

FEBRUARY 16

I LOVE

FEBRUARY 17

I LOVE

FEBRUARY 18

I LOVE

"GRATITUDE MAKES SENSE OF OUR PAST, BRINGS PEACE FOR TODAY, AND CREATES *a vision for tomorrow.*"

MELODY BEATTIE

FEBRUARY 19

I LOVE

FEBRUARY 20

I LOVE

FEBRUARY 21

I LOVE

FEBRUARY 22

I LOVE

"Love unlocks doors
AND OPENS WINDOWS THAT
WEREN'T EVEN THERE BEFORE."

MIGNON MCLAUGHLIN

FEBRUARY 23

I LOVE

FEBRUARY 24

I LOVE

FEBRUARY 25

I LOVE

_____

_____

_____

_____

_____

_____

_____

_____

_____

_____

FEBRUARY 26

I LOVE

_____

_____

_____

_____

_____

_____

_____

_____

_____

_____

FEBRUARY 27

I LOVE

FEBRUARY 28

I LOVE

FEBRUARY 29

I LOVE

FEBRUARY 30

I LOVE

MARCH

Character

NOT only can gratitude make us happy, it can make us good.
It can give us the courage to hold out our hand,
For there is no darkness in gratitude
And no light in its absence.

How can we comprehend this more clearly?
Try wadding up all bads into one wrap, labeled "self":
Selfish, Self-centered, Self-absorbed, Self-congratulating . . .
And notice that someone all wrapped up in himself
Makes a very small package.

Then on the opposite side of the box:
Empathy, humility, love, courage, honesty . . .
All flowing from gratitude.
Can you think of an evil person who was grateful?
Or of a proud, unappreciative one who was good?
Could it be that the mere practice of thanks-giving,
The deliberate effort to see through a gratitude lens,
Makes bad men good and good men better?
And gives us the honesty to be exactly who we are?

It is intuitive to know that loving more and thanking more
Lifts the receiver even as it builds the giver.
But just thinking about it won't do it.
It is the application that brings the accumulation.
Outflowing love and thanks creates the inflow
Of character.

THE CHALLENGE

THANKS and love,
One and one, one on one—each day
Say "thank you" to someone.
Not polite and perfunctory,
But eye-to-eye, or at least heart to heart,
Feeling it, meaning it.

Record the receiver's name,
Each day of the month, in this book.
And write down what you thanked them for.

MARCH 1

THANK YOU

MARCH 2

THANK YOU

"GRATITUDE IS THE SIGN OF NOBLE SOULS."

AESOP

MARCH 3

THANK YOU

MARCH 4

THANK YOU

MARCH 5

THANK YOU

MARCH 6

THANK YOU

"THERE IS NO GREATER
DIFFERENCE BETWEEN MEN THAN
between grateful
and ungrateful
people."

R. H. BLYTHE

MARCH 7

THANK YOU

_____
_____
_____
_____
_____
_____
_____
_____
_____
_____

MARCH 8

THANK YOU

_____
_____
_____
_____
_____
_____
_____
_____
_____

MARCH 9

THANK YOU

_____
_____
_____
_____
_____
_____
_____
_____
_____

MARCH 10

THANK YOU

_____
_____
_____
_____
_____
_____
_____
_____
_____

REPUTATION IS FOR TIME;
character is for
eternity.

J. B. GOUGH

MARCH 11

THANK YOU

MARCH 12

THANK YOU

MARCH 13

THANK YOU

MARCH 14

THANK YOU

"Gratitude is the greatest of virtues,

IN FACT, THE PARENT OF ALL OTHER VIRTUES."

CICERO

MARCH 15

THANK YOU

MARCH 16

THANK YOU

MARCH 17

THANK YOU

MARCH 18

THANK YOU

MARCH 19

THANK YOU

MARCH 20

THANK YOU

MARCH 21

THANK YOU

MARCH 22

THANK YOU

MARCH 23

THANK YOU

MARCH 24

THANK YOU

"NOTHING IS MORE HONORABLE THAN A grateful heart."

SENECA

MARCH 25

THANK YOU

MARCH 26

THANK YOU

MARCH 27

THANK YOU

MARCH 28

THANK YOU

MARCH 29

THANK YOU

MARCH 30

THANK YOU

MARCH 31

THANK YOU

APRIL

Asking

IF you are a parent, you want your children to ask.
Because the more they ask, the more likely they will be
To receive what you give.

And a wise child learns that to ask is to praise,
Which prompts the parent to give more.

The same equation and chemistry applies
With the parent that we call God,
And what foolish child would not avail himself
Of the source of exploding sunsets.
Asking is not the opposite of thanks-giving.
It is the complement and the other half of the formula.
Christ always coupled the equation:
"Ask and Receive."

In His universe (and it is His)
There is agency, and since that is His gift,
He does not violate it. If He were to
Take the initiative and simply give us what we need,
And what He would like to give (everything He has)
It would pilfer our agency and leave us
As dependent dole-dwellers.

So He commands "ask" because that is our initiative,
And the exercise of our agency
Leaves Him free to give without robbing
And to enrich our lives without impoverishing our will.

Some say "Don't ask too much" or "Don't ask for too much."
We say ask more and ask for more,
Because that is what God says, repeatedly, in holy writ.

"Ask"—may be the most frequently repeated admonition
In all of scripture.

Is redundancy a way of drumming its necessity?
Could failure to follow
Become our greatest eternal embarrassment?

But some children, asking constantly,
Prompt a parent to start saying "no."
Is it the same with God,
Or is there a built-in re-route switch
That circles our prayer back and alters and adjusts it,
Causing us to ask just what He wants us to,
Unlocking the very door He wants us to pass through,
Almost always a surprise;
And almost always, at least with later perspective,
Better.

Sometimes the best way to start is to just sit still,
cup your face, and relish the answers.

Be it God or one of His parent children,
There are some things no one gets tired of being asked:
Advice, Opinion, Input, Suggestions, Honest Questions.

Is asking weak, an admission of need, of dependency?
("If I have to ask directions, it admits I'm lost.")
No, it is the strong, honest, humble vulnerability
That invites love so that
Sometimes when we pray, our hearts know we are heard,
As though a hole opened into heaven.

THE CHALLENGE

SO this month, practice asking.
Practice the creative formulation of a good question.

Ask someone something, every day this month.
And in prayer, ask for one thing you truly think you need.
Write each day's mortal and divine question in this book,
Along with the answers you receive.
Notice the improvement in questions and answers
By month's end.

APRIL 1

ASKED SOMEONE

ASKED GOD

APRIL 2

ASKED SOMEONE

ASKED GOD

APRIL 3

ASKED SOMEONE

ASKED GOD

APRIL 4

ASKED SOMEONE

ASKED GOD

APRIL 5

ASKED SOMEONE

ASKED GOD

APRIL 6

ASKED SOMEONE

ASKED GOD

APRIL 7

ASKED SOMEONE

ASKED GOD

APRIL 8

ASKED SOMEONE

ASKED GOD

APRIL 9

ASKED SOMEONE

ASKED GOD

APRIL 10

ASKED SOMEONE

ASKED GOD

ASK, AND YE SHALL RECEIVE.

NEW TESTAMENT

APRIL 11

ASKED SOMEONE

ASKED GOD

APRIL 12

ASKED SOMEONE

ASKED GOD

APRIL 13

ASKED SOMEONE

ASKED GOD

APRIL 14

ASKED SOMEONE

ASKED GOD

"I WOULD RATHER BE ABLE TO *appreciate things* I CANNOT HAVE THAN TO HAVE THINGS I AM NOT ABLE TO APPRECIATE."

ELBERT HUBBARD

APRIL 15

ASKED SOMEONE

ASKED GOD

APRIL 16

ASKED SOMEONE

ASKED GOD

APRIL 17

ASKED SOMEONE

ASKED GOD

APRIL 18

ASKED SOMEONE

ASKED GOD

APRIL 19

ASKED SOMEONE

ASKED GOD

APRIL 20

ASKED SOMEONE

ASKED GOD

APRIL 21

ASKED SOMEONE

ASKED GOD

APRIL 22

ASKED SOMEONE

ASKED GOD

"Asking is the beginning

of receiving. Make sure

you don't go to the ocean

with a teaspoon."

JIM ROHN

APRIL 23

ASKED SOMEONE

ASKED GOD

APRIL 24

ASKED SOMEONE

ASKED GOD

APRIL 25

ASKED SOMEONE

ASKED GOD

APRIL 26

ASKED SOMEONE

ASKED GOD

"ASKING THE RIGHT QUESTIONS TAKES AS MUCH SKILL AS *giving the right answers.*"

ROBERT HALF

APRIL 27

ASKED SOMEONE

_____

_____

_____

_____

ASKED GOD

_____

_____

_____

_____

APRIL 28

ASKED SOMEONE

_____

_____

_____

_____

ASKED GOD

_____

_____

_____

_____

APRIL 29

ASKED SOMEONE

_____

_____

_____

_____

ASKED GOD

_____

_____

_____

_____

APRIL 30

ASKED SOMEONE

_____

_____

_____

_____

ASKED GOD

_____

_____

_____

_____

"IT IS NOT THE
ANSWER THAT ENLIGHTENS,
BUT THE QUESTION."

EUGENE IONESCO

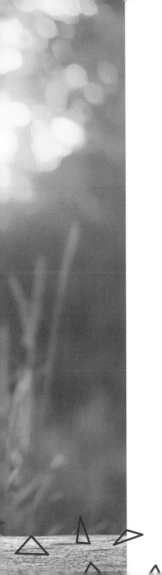

MAY

Receiving

LIFE ebbs and flows,
And at times the heavens seem to withdraw and withhold.
But there are other times when blessings swirl down
Like a flurry of blossoms and
We can neither grasp nor see them all.

But in feast and in famine, we need to learn how to receive.

Even in football, where Quarterbacks get the headlines,
None succeed without a good receiver.
No matter how perfect the pass,
Nothing counts if the receiver drops the ball.
Good receivers reach out and pull in,
Even as opposition swipes and bumps.

Good receivers never take the pass for granted
Or assume it will be easy to catch.
They expect difficulty and deal with it,
And they see the virtue even in a wobbly pass.

They are ready to run new routes and to adjust old ones
According to where the opposition lines up.
The more the receiver wants the ball and the more he
Shows his willingness to do whatever it takes to catch it,
The more the quarterback will pass to him.

The physics law says
Every action has an equal and opposite reaction.
Is there a corresponding spiritual law? Can there be?

In this world we borrow and owe and repay,
But we cannot repay heaven.
How do you repay breath or time or nature?
Are we hopelessly and eternally indebted?
And what could we return anyway?
What would you use as currency to pay back life?
As blessings come down, what can we send back up?

The only currency we have is thanks,
And maybe that will do . . . simply because the Lender
Already has everything else.
Perhaps our thanks is the appropriate and best return,
Since it is the only thing we have to give and the only thing
He does not have.

Receiving is a whole thing, an eternal round, encompassing.
Accept it all: The timing, The unexpected, The challenge
Never second-guessing, never doubting, never resenting—
Sometimes then, a flood of providence is unleashed,
Flowing unrestrained over every part of our world.

Ask and receive, give and take. Thus hold life in balance.
You will die if you don't take in a breath,
and you will die if you don't let it out.
All giving and no receiving may bring exhaustion,
Or resentment, or depression.
But all receiving and no giving is selfishness and entitlement.

In a universe where God owns all, receiving
Is more important than accomplishing and
Returning thanks is part of the celestial formula for returning.

Practice, persist,
Until receiving becomes an art, applicable equally
To the jewels around your neck or those clustered on a leaf.

THE CHALLENGE

SEND or deliver one hand-written note of thanks
Each week this month.
That alone will make you a unique receiver.
And since receiving is partly about accepting the
Balance between pleasure and pain,

In this book, each day, write two things:
The best and the worst, the happy and the sad.
Practice accepting them both,
Treating them both the same,
Finding some sliver or lining of joy in each.

MAY 1

HAPPY

SAD

MAY 2

HAPPY

SAD

"THE UNTHANKFUL HEART ...
DISCOVERS NO MERCIES; BUT LET
THE THANKFUL HEART SWEEP
THROUGH THE DAY AND, AS THE
MAGNET FINDS THE IRON, SO IT
WILL FIND, IN EVERY HOUR,
some heavenly blessings!"

HENRY WARD BEECHER

MAY 3

HAPPY

SAD

MAY 4

HAPPY

SAD

MAY 5

HAPPY

SAD

MAY 6

HAPPY

SAD

MAY 7

HAPPY

SAD

MAY 8

HAPPY

SAD

"TASTE IS NOTHING BUT AN ENLARGED CAPACITY FOR RECEIVING PLEASURE FROM WORKS OF IMAGINATION."

WILLIAM HAZLETT

MAY 9

HAPPY

SAD

MAY 10

HAPPY

SAD

MAY 11

HAPPY

SAD

MAY 12

HAPPY

SAD

MAY 13

HAPPY

SAD

MAY 14

HAPPY

SAD

MAY 15

HAPPY

SAD

MAY 16

HAPPY

SAD

MAY 17

HAPPY

SAD

MAY 18

HAPPY

SAD

"Hem your blessings WITH THANKFULNESS SO THEY DON'T UNRAVEL."

U N K N O W N

MAY 19

HAPPY

SAD

MAY 20

HAPPY

SAD

MAY 21

HAPPY

SAD

MAY 22

HAPPY

SAD

"IN ORDINARY LIFE WE HARDLY REALIZE THAT WE RECEIVE A GREAT DEAL MORE THAN WE GIVE, AND THAT *it is only with gratitude that life becomes rich.*"

DEITRICH BONHOEFFER

MAY 23

HAPPY

SAD

MAY 24

HAPPY

SAD

MAY 25

HAPPY

SAD

MAY 26

HAPPY

SAD

MAY 27

HAPPY

SAD

MAY 28

HAPPY

SAD

"FOR IT IS IN GIVING
THAT WE RECEIVE."

ST. FRANCIS OF ASSISI

MAY 29

HAPPY

SAD

MAY 30

HAPPY

SAD

MAY 31

HAPPY

SAD

JUNE

Health/Vitality

GRATITUDE is no passive lay-back,
It is a proactive grasp. Wherever you are,
Spin your head and count the blessings, the beach,
the light, the game, the vitality.
Popular phrase: "reinventing ourselves."
It might mean looking more deeply for our gifts
and our destinies.

But perhaps the best thing we can reinvent ourselves into
Is an always grateful person.
Which may prove to be the very fountain of vitality.

Vitality is health.
It is also purpose and meaning.
It is also thanks-giving.
For gratitude breeds vision and vigor and well-being
Which energizes and balances, inoculating against
The dark ills of depression and despair.
Gratitude is a positive emotion that strengthens its vessel.
A self-fulfilling prophecy
That seems to return more of whatever we give thanks for.

There is an abundance in gratitude, a billowing fullness
That warms and lifts us
And causes our bodies to respond with vigor,
Jumping high, through the world.

Besides fuel and rest, body well-being requires two things:
The exercise that tones the muscles and mind,
And the relaxation that calms them.

Gratitude can't do much directly for the former,
Although appreciation for activity may increase it,
But it can motivate and enhance the latter like nothing else.
Meditation or yoga or any kind of relaxation response
Is colored and textured by gratitude.

Especially if you alter your practice a bit. . . .

Instead of focusing on an object, focus on a blessing.
Instead of thinking about your breath,
Think with gratitude for air and lung.
Make "Thank You" your mantra

And the next time you hear about the proliferation of
Stress-induced illness,
You can counter it with your personal preservation of
Gratitude-induced vitality.

THE CHALLENGE

THIS month, once each day, anytime,
Pause.
Sit still and serene,
Close your eyes,
Relax and loosen wrists and ankles
And let it spread from there.

Then focus your mind for three minutes
On one simple, visualize-able blessing.
See it in your mind from all perspectives.
Block every other thought.
Later that day, write about that one thing in this book.

JUNE 1

_____

_____

_____

_____

_____

_____

_____

_____

_____

_____

JUNE 2

_____

_____

_____

_____

_____

_____

_____

_____

_____

_____

_____

JUNE 3

JUNE 4

""THE GROUNDWORK FOR ALL HAPPINESS IS HEALTH."

LEIGH HUNT

JUNE 5

JUNE 6

JUNE 7

JUNE 8

JUNE 9

JUNE 10

JUNE 11

JUNE 12

JUNE 13

JUNE 14

"GRATITUDE IS A VACCINE, AN ANTITOXIN, AND AN ANTISEPTIC."

JOHN HENRY JOWETT

JUNE 15

JUNE 16

JUNE 17

JUNE 18

JUNE 19

_____

_____

_____

_____

_____

_____

_____

_____

_____

JUNE 20

_____

_____

_____

_____

_____

_____

_____

_____

_____

_____

_____

JUNE 21

JUNE 22

"Gratitude unlocks the fullness of life.

IT TURNS WHAT WE HAVE INTO ENOUGH, AND MORE."

MELODIE BEATTIE

JUNE 23

JUNE 24

JUNE 25

JUNE 26

"EVERY ONE OF OUR GREATEST NATIONAL TREASURES, OUR LIBERTY, ENTERPRISE, VITALITY, WEALTH, MILITARY POWER, GLOBAL AUTHORITY, FLOW FROM A SURPRISING SOURCE: *our ability to give thanks.*"

TONY SNOW

JUNE 27

_____

_____

_____

_____

_____

_____

_____

_____

_____

_____

JUNE 28

_____

_____

_____

_____

_____

_____

_____

_____

_____

_____

_____

_____

JUNE 29

JUNE 30

"THERE ARE TWO KINDS OF GRATITUDE: THE SUDDEN KIND WE FEEL FOR WHAT WE TAKE; AND THE LARGER KIND WE FEEL FOR WHAT *we give.*"

EDWIN ARLINGTON ROBINSON

JULY

Family

GRATITUDE radiates from family like sparks
from flint and steel,
The One who lights our eye,
and the children that light our lives.

No family is perfect,
All families have challenges, but
Commitment is what cements family joy . . .
As we grasp the foreverness of family and feel
The security of saying "It is you, and it will always be you."
Gratitude floods in.
The harsh uncertainty of the outside world
Is neutralized by the sureness and security
Of the inside home
Where we celebrate commitment and popularize parenting
And validate values.

Then we venture forth strong into the outer
Because of the inner gratitude we carry always with us.

For partners, thanks-giving's lens focuses light,
White hot, on the precise center of the gratitude bulls eye.
The One. Our other half. The burning focal point of love,
The blessing above all blessings.

Saying "I love you more than all else, and more than myself"
Is like saying "My ultimate thanks is for you and to you."
No greater love, no greater gratitude.
Neither can be said too often.
And nothing can provide more power and more peace.
For parents, thanks-giving
Is not only our reward but our methodology
Because gratitude is the antidote to the entitlement attitudes
That would destroy our families and our kids.

Children, particularly young, unspoiled ones,
Possess the natural gift of gratitude—but it is unlit.
We can spark it, not by telling them to say thank you
But by letting them see us say it, repeatedly, all day,
To friends, to teachers, to God, and even to them.

The more they hear you say it,
And see your happiness as you do,
The more they will emulate both the saying and the feeling.

Start with the conscious realization that family matters most.
Real Eyes that most things we do are merely the means
For the same end.
And that end is family.
Sort the means from the ends with one simple question:
"Why?"
Why do you work? Why do you strive?
Why do you pray? Why do you eat? Why do you care?
Ultimately, the answer to every why is "family."

Would there be a parallel ratio between how much
You value a thing and how grateful you are for it?
(Level of importance proportionate to level of thanks?)

If so, no contest. We are most grateful for family.
But gratitude and joy do not linger like a heavy blanket,
Rather they come in flashes, in moments,
And we recognize them as a gleam in the eye.

THE CHALLENGE

THIS month,
Guided by your imagination and your hope,
Write a one-paragraph description of your relationship
With each member of your family five years from now.

This is relationship goal-setting,
And it can become self-fulfilling, a verbal magnet
That pulls reality
And sparks the most personal gratitude of all.

DESCRIPTION OF MY RELATIONSHIP WITH _____
FIVE YEARS FROM TODAY

_____

_____

_____

_____

_____

_____

_____

_____

_____

_____

_____

DESCRIPTION OF MY RELATIONSHIP WITH _____
FIVE YEARS FROM TODAY

_____

_____

_____

_____

_____

_____

_____

_____

_____

_____

_____

DESCRIPTION OF MY RELATIONSHIP WITH _____
FIVE YEARS FROM TODAY

_____
_____
_____
_____
_____
_____
_____
_____
_____
_____
_____
_____

DESCRIPTION OF MY RELATIONSHIP WITH _____
FIVE YEARS FROM TODAY

_____
_____
_____
_____
_____
_____
_____
_____
_____
_____
_____

DESCRIPTION OF MY RELATIONSHIP WITH _____
FIVE YEARS FROM TODAY

_____

_____

_____

_____

_____

_____

_____

_____

_____

_____

_____

DESCRIPTION OF MY RELATIONSHIP WITH _____
FIVE YEARS FROM TODAY

_____

_____

_____

_____

_____

_____

_____

_____

_____

_____

_____

"HOW WONDERFUL IT WOULD BE IF WE COULD HELP OUR CHILDREN AND GRANDCHILDREN to learn thanksgiving AT AN EARLY AGE."

SIR JOHN TEMPLETON

DESCRIPTION OF MY RELATIONSHIP WITH _____
FIVE YEARS FROM TODAY

_____

_____

_____

_____

_____

_____

_____

_____

_____

_____

_____

DESCRIPTION OF MY RELATIONSHIP WITH _____
FIVE YEARS FROM TODAY

_____

_____

_____

_____

_____

_____

_____

_____

_____

_____

DESCRIPTION OF MY RELATIONSHIP WITH _____
FIVE YEARS FROM TODAY

_____

_____

_____

_____

_____

_____

_____

_____

_____

DESCRIPTION OF MY RELATIONSHIP WITH _____
FIVE YEARS FROM TODAY

_____

_____

_____

_____

_____

_____

_____

_____

_____

"HOW SHARPER THAN A SERPENT'S TOOTH IT IS TO HAVE A THANKLESS CHILD!"

WILLIAM SHAKESPEARE,
KING LEAR

DESCRIPTION OF MY RELATIONSHIP WITH _____
FIVE YEARS FROM TODAY

_____
_____
_____
_____
_____
_____
_____
_____
_____
_____
_____

DESCRIPTION OF MY RELATIONSHIP WITH _____
FIVE YEARS FROM TODAY

_____
_____
_____
_____
_____
_____
_____
_____
_____
_____

DESCRIPTION OF MY RELATIONSHIP WITH _____
FIVE YEARS FROM TODAY

_____

_____

_____

_____

_____

_____

_____

_____

_____

_____

_____

DESCRIPTION OF MY RELATIONSHIP WITH _____
FIVE YEARS FROM TODAY

_____

_____

_____

_____

_____

_____

_____

_____

_____

_____

_____

DESCRIPTION OF MY RELATIONSHIP WITH _____
FIVE YEARS FROM TODAY

_____

_____

_____

_____

_____

_____

_____

_____

_____

_____

_____

_____

DESCRIPTION OF MY RELATIONSHIP WITH _____
FIVE YEARS FROM TODAY

_____

_____

_____

_____

_____

_____

_____

_____

_____

_____

_____

_____

DESCRIPTION OF MY RELATIONSHIP WITH _____
FIVE YEARS FROM TODAY

_____

_____

_____

_____

_____

_____

_____

_____

_____

_____

_____

DESCRIPTION OF MY RELATIONSHIP WITH _____
FIVE YEARS FROM TODAY

_____

_____

_____

_____

_____

_____

_____

_____

_____

_____

DESCRIPTION OF MY RELATIONSHIP WITH _____
FIVE YEARS FROM TODAY

_____

_____

_____

_____

_____

_____

_____

_____

_____

_____

_____

DESCRIPTION OF MY RELATIONSHIP WITH _____
FIVE YEARS FROM TODAY

_____

_____

_____

_____

_____

_____

_____

_____

_____

_____

_____

DESCRIPTION OF MY RELATIONSHIP WITH _____
FIVE YEARS FROM TODAY

_____

_____

_____

_____

_____

_____

_____

_____

_____

_____

_____

DESCRIPTION OF MY RELATIONSHIP WITH _____
FIVE YEARS FROM TODAY

_____

_____

_____

_____

_____

_____

_____

_____

_____

_____

_____

"A HAPPY FAMILY IS BUT
an earlier heaven."

GEORGE BERNARD SHAW

DESCRIPTION OF MY RELATIONSHIP WITH _____
FIVE YEARS FROM TODAY

_____

_____

_____

_____

_____

_____

_____

_____

_____

_____

_____

_____

DESCRIPTION OF MY RELATIONSHIP WITH _____
FIVE YEARS FROM TODAY

_____

_____

_____

_____

_____

_____

_____

_____

_____

_____

_____

"THE FAMILY IS ONE OF nature's masterpieces."

GEORGE SANTAYANA

DESCRIPTION OF MY RELATIONSHIP WITH _____
FIVE YEARS FROM TODAY

_____

_____

_____

_____

_____

_____

_____

_____

_____

_____

DESCRIPTION OF MY RELATIONSHIP WITH _____
FIVE YEARS FROM TODAY

_____

_____

_____

_____

_____

_____

_____

_____

_____

DESCRIPTION OF MY RELATIONSHIP WITH _____
FIVE YEARS FROM TODAY

_____
_____
_____
_____
_____
_____
_____
_____
_____
_____

DESCRIPTION OF MY RELATIONSHIP WITH _____
FIVE YEARS FROM TODAY

_____
_____
_____
_____
_____
_____
_____
_____
_____
_____

DESCRIPTION OF MY RELATIONSHIP WITH _____
FIVE YEARS FROM TODAY

_____

_____

_____

_____

_____

_____

_____

_____

_____

_____

DESCRIPTION OF MY RELATIONSHIP WITH _____
FIVE YEARS FROM TODAY

_____

_____

_____

_____

_____

_____

_____

_____

_____

_____

DESCRIPTION OF MY RELATIONSHIP WITH _____
FIVE YEARS FROM TODAY

_____
_____
_____
_____
_____
_____
_____
_____
_____
_____
_____

AUGUST

Adversity

MANY of us, with the blessing of hindsight, say
Thank you for adversity and conclude
that the greatest moments were when lightning struck.

Looking back, we can see
How something we thought was horrible and unfair
Turned out to be a great blessing.

The trick is to see it that way right away!
In a sense, adversity is essential to gratitude.
If there were none of one there would be none of the other.
Light can't be seen without the contrast of dark.

Adversity projects its own kind of beauty,
Too hot to touch, but
Bathing our faces in flickering light,
Helping us to understand how strong and how beautiful
We really are.

Sometimes it hits us in the face,
And other times we see it coming out of the corner of our eye.

There are two correct responses to adversity
Depending on its nature.
One is to fight it and change it and win out over it.
The other is to accept it and summon gratitude for it.
Separating the two
Is one of the most valuable skills in life;
Some people call it "picking your battles."

Sometimes the mere act of being thankful for adversity
Takes the sting out of it.
Whistle while you work. Sing as you march into battle.
A little known Biblical king, Josiah, overshadowed by
Luminaries like David and Solomon, practiced this with success.
When a large allied army swept down on tiny Israel,
Josiah placed his choir at the front of his army, singing,
"Give thanks to the Lord for he is good.
His mercy endures forever."
The opposing force became disoriented and fled in terror.

Adversity is the best atmosphere in which to practice gratitude
. . . like the resistance on the treadmill
. . . like a kite rising against the wind.

THE CHALLENGE

THIS month, actually audit your adversity,
Not to emphasize the negative,
But to prove to yourself that it's a necessary part
That is always there.
Instead of hoping to be rid of it,
Make peace with it, and hone the art of overcoming.

In this book, each day,
Note some little obstacle you faced,
And write how you either got past it
Or made friends with it.

AUGUST 1

OBSTACLE

WHAT I DID WITH IT

AUGUST 2

OBSTACLE

WHAT I DID WITH IT

"BEING MISTREATED IS THE MOST IMPORTANT CONDITION OF MORTALITY, *for eternity itself* DEPENDS ON HOW WE VIEW THOSE WHO MISTREAT US."

JAMES L. FERRELL

AUGUST 3

OBSTACLE

WHAT I DID WITH IT

AUGUST 4

OBSTACLE

WHAT I DID WITH IT

AUGUST 5

OBSTACLE

WHAT I DID WITH IT

AUGUST 6

OBSTACLE

WHAT I DID WITH IT

"WHEN IT IS DARK ENOUGH,

*you can see
the stars.*"

RALPH WALDO EMERSON

AUGUST 7

OBSTACLE

WHAT I DID WITH IT

AUGUST 8

OBSTACLE

WHAT I DID WITH IT

AUGUST 9

OBSTACLE

WHAT I DID WITH IT

AUGUST 10

OBSTACLE

WHAT I DID WITH IT

"I DON'T EMBRACE TROUBLE;
THAT'S AS BAD AS TREATING IT
AS AN ENEMY. BUT I DO SAY

meet it as a friend,

FOR YOU WILL SEE A LOT OF
IT, AND HAD BETTER BE ON
SPEAKING TERMS WITH IT."

OLIVER WENDELL HOLMES

AUGUST 11

OBSTACLE

WHAT I DID WITH IT

AUGUST 12

OBSTACLE

WHAT I DID WITH IT

AUGUST 13

OBSTACLE

WHAT I DID WITH IT

AUGUST 14

OBSTACLE

WHAT I DID WITH IT

"THERE IS NO EDUCATION LIKE ADVERSITY."

BENJAMIN DISRAELI

AUGUST 15

OBSTACLE

WHAT I DID WITH IT

AUGUST 16

OBSTACLE

WHAT I DID WITH IT

AUGUST 17

OBSTACLE

WHAT I DID WITH IT

AUGUST 18

OBSTACLE

WHAT I DID WITH IT

AUGUST 19

OBSTACLE

WHAT I DID WITH IT

AUGUST 20

OBSTACLE

WHAT I DID WITH IT

AUGUST 21

OBSTACLE

WHAT I DID WITH IT

AUGUST 22

OBSTACLE

WHAT I DID WITH IT

AUGUST 23

OBSTACLE

WHAT I DID WITH IT

AUGUST 24

OBSTACLE

WHAT I DID WITH IT

"WHEN WRITTEN IN CHINESE, THE WORD *CRISIS* IS COMPOSED OF TWO CHARACTERS—ONE REPRESENTS DANGER, AND THE OTHER

represents opportunity."

JOHN F. KENNEDY

AUGUST 25

OBSTACLE

WHAT I DID WITH IT

AUGUST 26

OBSTACLE

WHAT I DID WITH IT

AUGUST 27

OBSTACLE

WHAT I DID WITH IT

AUGUST 28

OBSTACLE

WHAT I DID WITH IT

AUGUST 29

OBSTACLE

WHAT I DID WITH IT

AUGUST 30

OBSTACLE

WHAT I DID WITH IT

AUGUST 31

OBSTACLE

WHAT I DID WITH IT

SEPTEMBER

Serendipity/Stewardship

WE often resist something that we should relish
And be grateful for.
It is the unexpected.
Surprise, well accepted, is the spice and savor of life.
Not knowing where the river winds or
Where the day will take you is a reality
That we might as well convert into a joy.

And, opposite, we often relish something that we should resist.
It is the notion of ownership.
We don't own anything, except perhaps our agency.
All else passes through our hands, owned only by God
And loaned to us on trial.
As much as we might think we want control,
The best we can hope for is serendipity,
And our misplaced pursuit of ownership

Converts with wisdom to stewardship.
Together, these two 11-letter "S" words
Give us a guided glimpse of divine gratitude.

Serendipity and Stewardship, like Scripture, tell us to focus
On Watching and Praying at least as much as on
Working and Planning, because
Along will come something better than
What we thought we pursued;
And while nothing is ours, all is given to us.

Thus real joy comes not just in the striving
But in the accepting,
And sometimes just to leap and soar,
Trusting that you will land where you should.
Let's push back the Working and Planning,
And the other Worldly and Posturing W and P words
Worry and Pursue
Wealth and Power, and even
Writing and Prose.

To make room for a new gratitude-freshened W and P set:
Watch and Pray
Wander and Ponder
Wonder and Probe
Worship and Praise
Waken and Perceive
Wait and Procrastinate (selectively)
Weigh and Perspective
Wisdom and Peace, and even
Watching and Poetry

Then, like a steward, we will begin to see serendipity,
Then, like a baby, we will crawl pleasantly
Into the unknown.

THE CHALLENGE

GIVE up on control.
Write down each day something that
You are glad you don't consciously control
From things as internally automatic as digestion or
Your tear ducts or sweat glands—
To something as unpredictably external as weather
Or sunsets.

Think how glad you are to observe and enjoy and benefit
Rather than controlling them all.

SEPTEMBER 1

SEPTEMBER 2

"Gratitude is a quality

SIMILAR TO ELECTRICITY. IT MUST BE PRODUCED AND DISCHARGED AND USED UP IN ORDER TO EXIST AT ALL."

WILLIAM FAULKNER

SEPTEMBER 3

_____

_____

_____

_____

_____

_____

_____

_____

_____

_____

SEPTEMBER 4

_____

_____

_____

_____

_____

_____

_____

_____

_____

_____

SEPTEMBER 5

SEPTEMBER 6

"THE ROBBED THAT SMILES
STEALS SOMETHING
FROM THE THIEF."

WILLIAM SHAKESPEARE,
OTHELLO

SEPTEMBER 7

SEPTEMBER 8

SEPTEMBER 9

SEPTEMBER 10

SEPTEMBER 11

SEPTEMBER 12

SEPTEMBER 13

SEPTEMBER 14

"NOTHING IS POSSESSED SAVE IN APPRECIATION, OF WHICH THANKFULNESS IS THE INDISPENSABLE INGREDIENT. But a thankful heart hath a continual feast."

W. J. CAMERON

SEPTEMBER 15

SEPTEMBER 16

SEPTEMBER 17

SEPTEMBER 18

"Gratitude shifts your focus FROM WHAT YOUR LIFE LACKS TO THE ABUNDANCE THAT IS ALREADY PRESENT."

MARELISA FABREGA

SEPTEMBER 19

SEPTEMBER 20

SEPTEMBER 21

SEPTEMBER 22

"SERENDIPITY IS THE FACULTY
OF FINDING THINGS
*we did not know we
were looking for.*"

GLAUCO ORTOLANO

SEPTEMBER 23

SEPTEMBER 24

SEPTEMBER 25

SEPTEMBER 26

SEPTEMBER 27

SEPTEMBER 28

SEPTEMBER 29

SEPTEMBER 30

OCTOBER

The Confident Humility of Faith

THE acceptance of God as the Giver
Makes us strive for excellence, but also
Allows us to relax and just be who we are.

Among other wonders is the wonder of smallness—
The miracle that we are exactly the right size for the earth.
We fit the scale.
Were we bigger or smaller,
We would not work well with this world.
Spiritually it is the same—
As His creations, we are among the tiniest,
As His children, we are of largest import and consequence.

It is somewhat sad
That two symbiotic, nearly synonymous words
Are thought of as opposites. . . .
Humility and confidence look like each other's antithesis
Until their common source—our relationship to God—
is revealed and they
Coalesce into closeness and simpatico,
Pushed together by perspective, and by
A father who helps us stand.

If we call God "Father," and mean it,
We merit inescapable, inherited confidence,
Yet His perfection's vast distance from our foibles
Creates profound humility

A relaxing quality that puts the pressure off of you
And the yoke on Him.

The message: Stop stressing and start praying.

To a Christian, there is one form of thanks
That supersedes and overpowers all others.
It is the unspeakable, un-repayable, unfathomable gratitude
We feel to a Savior who has literally purchased us
With His blood.

Somehow—some ungraspable how—
He had amassed enough spiritual capital
To ransom us, to pay the staggering debt of our
Collective sin and error
And allow us to escape the debtors prison into which
We would otherwise find ourselves eternally confined.

One reason this gratitude goes beyond all others
Is that Christ's ultimate gift is something that neither we,
Nor anyone else who has ever lived,
Could have done for ourselves.

And while we cannot fully comprehend it,
We can stand in awe, which is the ultimate gratitude.
As C. S. Lewis said, "Beware of professed Christians
Who posses insufficient awe of Christ."
Or as Neal A. Maxwell expanded, "The more we ponder
Where we stand in relation to Jesus Christ,
The more we realize
That we do not stand at all, we only kneel."

Without this gift, our lives would be much like
A diminishing road into a growing fog,
Or like a dying red sun setting in for the last time.
But with His gift, the fog dissipates, the sun rises again,
And we are free to recover, time and time again
And to continually partake of all the lesser blessings.

THE CHALLENGE

CULTIVATE a positive "can't do" attitude.
Oxymoron?
No, because the *can't do* is the realistic humility
Of how inconsequential we are,
While the positive is the spiritualistic faith
Of how God can do with us and through us, anything.

Each day write down
Something you have that you don't deserve and didn't earn.
This, by the way,
Is the very easiest of all twelve challenges.

OCTOBER 1

OCTOBER 2

"I AM NOTHING; I AM BUT AN INSTRUMENT, A TINY PENCIL IN THE HANDS OF THE LORD WITH WHICH HE WRITES WHAT HE LIKES. HOWEVER IMPERFECT WE ARE, HE WRITES BEAUTIFULLY."

MOTHER TERESA

OCTOBER 3

OCTOBER 4

OCTOBER 5

OCTOBER 6

"The earth is the Lord's AND EVERYTHING IN IT."

PSALMS 24:1

OCTOBER 7

OCTOBER 8

OCTOBER 9

OCTOBER 10

OCTOBER 11

OCTOBER 12

OCTOBER 13

OCTOBER 14

OCTOBER 15

OCTOBER 16

"GOD HAS TWO DWELLINGS: ONE IN HEAVEN, AND THE OTHER IN A *meek and thankful heart.*"

IZAAK WALTON

OCTOBER 17

OCTOBER 18

"Without humility
IT IS IMPOSSIBLE TO ENJOY
ANYTHING, EVEN PRIDE."

G. K. CHESTERTON

OCTOBER 19

OCTOBER 20

OCTOBER 21

OCTOBER 22

OCTOBER 23

OCTOBER 24

OCTOBER 25

OCTOBER 26

"'Thank you'
IS THE BEST PRAYER THAT
ANYONE COULD SAY. I SAY
THAT ONE A LOT. THANK
YOU EXPRESSES EXTREME
GRATITUDE, HUMILITY,
UNDERSTANDING."

ALICE WALKER

OCTOBER 27

OCTOBER 28

OCTOBER 29

OCTOBER 30

OCTOBER 31

ABOUT THE AUTHORS

RICHARD AND LINDA EYRE are the authors of more than 50 books that have been translated into a dozen languages and sold in the millions. Their speaking website is TheEyres.com, and their parenting and family programs are at valuesparenting.com. The Eyres do a Thanksgiving greeting card each year. You can view past cards at www.valuesparenting.com/thanksgiving and can receive the new card each November by adding your name to the mailing list there.

OTHER FAMILIUS BOOKS
BY THE EYRES

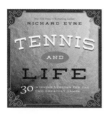

TENNIS AND LIFE: 30 Winning Lessons for the Two Greatest Games
Bestselling author and tennis champion Richard Eyre explains why, of all sports, tennis is the best metaphor for life. He then shares thirty principles that will help you enjoy both games more—and play both games better.

GRANDMOTHERING: The Secrets to Making a Difference While Having the Time of Your Life
Linda shares her secret formula for teaching your grandchildren values, building meaningful connections with them, and giving them grit and resilience, plus an appendix of easy recipes to feed a crowd.

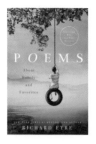

POEMS: About Family and Favorites: Exploring Who and What We Love
Here, for the first time in published form, Richard Eyre shares some of his most poetic efforts for those who have enjoyed his prose, and for those who haven't. None who know Richard will be surprised that most of his poems connect to family.

BEING A PROACTIVE GRANDFATHER: How to Make a Difference

Richard Eyre encourages those of us whose children have had children to ask ourselves a very important question: "what kind of grandfather will you be?" The two key words in the title are BEING and GRAND. A great book for grandmothers to give to their husbands!

THE HAPPINESS PARADOX: The Very Things We Thought Would Bring Us Joy Actually Steal It Away

Richard contends that the three things today's society desires the most—control, ownership, and independence—are, paradoxically, the three things that bring the most challenges and unhappiness in our lives. Read this book from one side for the problem of the paradox, and then read it from the other side for the solution of the paradigm.

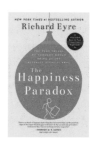

THE HALF-DIET DIET: The Guaranteed Weight-Loss Program That Reboots Your Body, Mind, and Spirit for a Happier Life

More than just a weight-loss program, *The Half-Diet Diet* helps you meet your weight-loss goals by taming your physical, mental, and spiritual appetites. The Eyres' promise: "The weight you lose will be the least of the rewards that appetite-control will bring."

THE 8 MYTHS OF MARRIAGING: Making Marriage a Verb and Replacing Myth with Truth

Exploring equality versus synergy, completion versus individual quest, harmony versus productive debate, a test drive versus constant commitment, and more, the Eyres show that eight popular opinions and behaviors toward successful marriages actually reduce the chance of marriage fulfillment.

LIFE IN FULL: Maximizing Your Longevity and Legacy

A seven-question blueprint for ho`w to spend the next twenty years living the life you have always wanted and enjoying the life fulfillment you deserve. This is a book written for Baby Boomers who want to make the "Autumn" of their lives their best season, and who want to prioritize family relationships more than ever before.

THE TURNING: Why the State of the Family Matters, and What the World Can Do About It

In the spirit of Friedman's *The World Is Flat*, Richard and Linda Eyre examine the connections between the world's mounting social problems and the breakdown of families and look deeply at the root causes of family disintegration. Then, in the second half of the book, the Eyres suggest macro solutions for society and micro solutions and practical parenting ideas for parents inside their own homes.

BY ORDERING DIRECTLY
FROM FAMILIUS,
YOU CAN GET THE EYRES'
OTHER BOOKS FOR 40% OFF!

JUST VISIT
FAMILIUS.COM/EYRES-SPECIAL
AND USE THE ACCESS CODE
FAMILIUSFRIEND.

ENJOY!

ABOUT FAMILIUS

FAMILIUS is a global trade publishing company that publishes books and other content to help families be happy. We believe that the family is the fundamental unit of society and that happy families are the foundation of a happy life. We recognize that every family looks different, and we passionately believe in helping all families find greater joy. To that end, we publish books for children and adults that invite families to live the Familius Nine Habits of Happy Family Life: *love together, play together, learn together, work together, talk together, heal together, read together, eat together,* and *laugh together.* Founded in 2012, Familius is located in Sanger, California.

CONNECT

Website: www.familius.com
Facebook: www.facebook.com/paterfamilius
Twitter: @familiustalk, @paterfamilius1
Pinterest: www.pinterest.com/familius
Instagram: @familiustalk

The most important work you ever do will be within the walls of your own home.